Self- Destructive Behaviors,
Self- Injury and Nonsuicidal Self- Injury:
A Therapists' Guide for Family Work and Support

AuthorHouse™
1663 Liberty Drive
Bloomington, IN 47403
www.authorhouse.com
Phone: 1-800-839-8640

First published by AuthorHouse 10/15/09

ISBN: 978-1-4490-2243-3 (e)
ISBN: 978-1-4490-2241-9 (sc)

Library of Congress Control Number: 2009910960

Printed in the United States of America
Bloomington, Indiana

This book is printed on acid-free paper.

Self- Destructive Behaviors,
Self- Injury and Nonsuicidal Self- Injury:

A Therapists' Guide for Family Work and Support

K. R. Juzwin, Psy.D.

A Guide to Help Those Who Love Someone Who Self-Injures

Acknowledgments

This book, along with its sister journal text, was written to help therapists working with people who are struggling with self-destructive behaviors and want to change their lives and need a component to help with the family/significant-other piece. Self-injury and self-destructive behaviors can become such a big part of life and relationships, that the thought of change is overwhelming. This is a long process, one that many people don't understand, and will ask not just the person, but their entire family and social network to change with them.

This book was written as a result of discussions with clinicians about their own case loads and asking for ideas of managing the patient and their families. Indeed, this consultation process is the way therapists keep learning, we ask for ideas, and share what does and doesn't work. I have had the great privilege of learning from and with some outstanding clinicians and teachers. I am a product of the construct of "social contribution" which is an Adlerian term, which reflects the importance of shared learning, contributing and support. To that, I have many people who have helped me in this process. First and foremost, the patients and families who have let me walk with them, and included me on their journeys. They are the most courageous people I've ever met.

Professional education and mentoring has been a long and ongoing process, and I too am a student of myself. I have had the privilege of learning from some of the best in this regard through my experiences with my colleagues and mentors at Alexian Brothers Behavioral Health Hospital and my colleagues in private practices, Alternatives Center and The Art of Living. Annmarie Belmonte and Kathy Zachary, thank you for your encouragement in this project, and the time, effort and generous feedback about this work. I also thank my colleagues at Alexian Brothers Self-Injury Recovery Services at who have encouraged me in my consultation, teaching and supervisory work, above and beyond my clinical work. The work they do is extraordinary, and they are superb at their craft.

Because this is a handbook focusing on families, I think it is important to include a comment to my own family, extended, and adopted friend/family members. Each of these people understands and shares the importance of family and values, and living those values in all they do. I was fortunate to be raised in a home where parents believed that parenting was about preparing your children to live in the world responsibly and contributing manner, and did their best to model this. They believed we were capable of and responsible for being self-efficacious and contributing, and they held those standards, and taught us how. We knew what we as a family stood for and valued. My father believed family was the most important obligation we have, and upheld this in his life. I will forever hear his guidance and encouragement in my mind. I have tried, with the help of others who support me, to be that for my own family, child and children in my life. To that, I try parent with a very simple credo: I try to behave as a model for what skills I want them to develop themselves, and try not to behave in a way that I would be embarrassed or ashamed to explain to my child or family. I want my family to know they are both my foundation for living and my framework and guiding lights. Thank you. krj

Index

Instructions and Requests for the Family

Note to the Client/Patient/Family Member: If you have someone in your family, or you are a friend of someone, who is harming themselves through any form of self-injury, this guide is to use as part of the *therapy work with your family therapist*.

If you are struggling with self-injury or other kinds of self-destructive behaviors, please work with a therapist while working on this journal. It is not recommended that you work without extra support and guidance of a therapist. If you are working with a therapist or counselor, follow their recommendations and their lead. Each page has a specific lesson or message. The goal is to work slowly, learning each lesson, and connecting your mind and body in the present. Your therapist will help you learn how to not be overwhelmed and to keep you safe.

Please don't use this without discussing it with a therapist to help you understand the behavior and thinking patterns and offer information about how to help them in the process as they work to change this. It is important that you understand how important you can be in the successful recovery process, but doing these exercises without the help of a professional is not recommended. In some cases, things may become even worse. Please don't just copy these exercises and use them without guidance by a therapist who has everyone's best interest in mind.

Unfortunately, this problem is about more than the behavior and thinking patterns. It involves many changes in the entire family, as well as with friends and in activities. Families often need support to help this happen, that is why the recommendation for family involvement is so important. Everybody will change because of this. The person you care about needs to have the most important people in their life support the work they are doing in therapy. Sometimes things get worse before they get better, and sometimes they just get worse. Working with a therapist will help increase the chance that things will get better.

You will see what is written here focuses on family relationships and parenting. This is not to criticize the family or parenting in any way, but a guide to help those people with the most power (the parents) create a place (home) where children can become healthy people. Parenting is hard, and parenting children and teens with problem behaviors is very difficult. This is a guide to offer support for those who are willing to see themselves as part of the recovery process for the person you love.

Before you read any more, it is important to understand something about self-destructive behaviors and recovery from them:

Self-injury is not just about the behavior.

Recovery from self-injury involves changing how one relates to themselves, other people, and their world.

It is about changing the rules of living.

It is about taking the opportunities to teach and to learn something new.

About treatment......

- It involves change.
- It involves changing how we relate to ourselves, our body, other people, and the world around us.
- It involves choosing different behaviors and beliefs.
- It involves learning to tolerate feelings.
- It involves willingness to have values.
- It involves being willing to see yourself as having worth and value, and being worthy of self-respect.
- It involves your commitment to practicing being safe, secure and physically well.
- It involves making decisions based on what is healthy and age-appropriate, not based on what we want.
- It involves time.
- It involves ups and downs, successes and struggles.
- It will involve looking at family rules, roles, values and lessons.
- It will involve challenging maladaptive patterns of behavior.
- It involves new patterns of behaviors and relating to people.

So to answer the question about what you can do:

- Understand that the behavior is only one part of the problem. It also involves the thinking, feeling and reacting.
- Understand that the behavior serves a function or purpose to the person.
- Understand that self-injury is not the same as suicide.
- Understand the recommendations made by professionals.
- Understand that there are real mental health problems involved here.
- People who self-injure are people with problems staying alive and coping.
- They are not their problems or their behaviors; please don't call them "cutters."
- People who self-injure can rotate through symptoms. If the underlying problem doesn't change, the behavior may rotate through different phases.
- Understand that the process of change takes time.
- Consider development and maturation factors as people grow and age.
- Look for opportunities to teach the behaviors and lessons that are important.
- Foster an environment for success.
- Look for opportunities to give encouragement and positive feedback.
- Think your way through problems and manage your emotions appropriately.
- Take a time out to think about the problem, cool off, and then go back and set the limits and resolve the problem. You don't have to go to every battle you are invited to.
- Accept that there may need to be some changes in your own household.
- Accept that the entire family may need to change the way you interact or deal with the person.
- Consider the importance of healthy limits, boundaries and expectations as a foundation for health.
- Understand the importance of taking care of the whole body, the whole person.

- You may have to consider how you relate to people, and your friends, family and other relationships.
- Consider yourself part of the treatment support team, participate, learn, and teach.
- You may have to consider changing activities and patterns.
- It involves active, honest, and consistent participation in treatment.
- Be mindful of how powerful your actions are in teaching children about life.
- Think your way through your relationships, it will be much more peaceful, calm and rational than being emotional and reactive
- Think about your impact on those around you, are you getting the reactions you need?
- Keep in mind the goal is to RAISE A HEALTHY CHILD!
- Asking for support is a good thing.

When you practice and talk about the activities in this book, you are helping because you are teaching:
- Language skills for communication and expression.
- How to interact, get their needs met appropriately.
- How to tolerate frustration.
- How to tolerate having to ask for help appropriately.
- How to tolerate getting helped.
- How to tolerate interaction and closeness.
- How to ask questions and think about things, and then sit with them.
- It is an opportunity to have healthy mentoring interactions which help with attachment, modeling and social skills.
- It is an opportunity to build off of their existing skills, intelligence and resources.
- Have an opportunity to teach values.
- Have an opportunity to model appropriate mentor/teacher/parent behavior, where there is a hierarchy that isn't about pain and power, but about learning appropriate social cues, social conventions and appropriate social interaction.
- It is a teaching opportunity!

Basic parenting concepts to help raise healthy kids:
- It is more important to be a RESPONSIBLE parent than to be the "cool parent" or a "fun parent." This is irresponsible.
- Your home is the first world where they learn to be social skills, self-management skills, values, expectations and accountability. Waiting for them to learn these skills outside of the home is too late.
- The goal of parenting is to raise healthy kids, not "happy" kids.
- Kids need rules, structure and routine.
- Kids do better with limits and known expectations.
- Kids need to have accountability, structure, and feedback about their behaviors and choices. This is how kids learn how to govern their behaviors and learn self-discipline.

- The job of a kid is to test the rules, the job of a parent is to set the rules and enforce them. Without this, children don't learn this, and struggle later on in structured settings like school and work.
- Privileges are earned based on maturity and the kids' ability to manage them.
- Part of growing up is testing the limits; part of growing up is hearing the word "NO" when those limits have been pushed.
- Limits help teach a number of important self-management lesson.
- Kids learn from watching others.
- Your ACTIONS teach far more than your lectures.
- Rewards and privileges should only be at the level your kid can handle them. You know this by their appropriate behaviors and self-management.
- Parents need to give feedback, letting kids know when they are doing a good job, and encouraging them to make good choices (and let them know when they do it!).
- Riding in the car is a great time to talk, put your cell phones down!
- Family meals and activities are important times to come together as a family.
- The best parenting is done when it is done with logic, contained emotions and from the desire to teach and stand by your limits and expectations.
- The best parenting is done when a parent models and practices being what they want their child to be.

Instructions and Request for the Therapist & Counselor

Note for the Therapist & Counselor: This book is a set of exercises for therapists to use in therapy with patients/clients who self-injure to help with the family work.

Our role as a treatment provider includes several goals. These goals include providing education, information, consultation and support for community services. It also is important to include family and other supportive people when necessary and appropriate. Then, to take it a step farther, have the patient/client help teach supportive family members these important self-management skills. This is a teaching, support, and modeling approach.

A necessary part of treatment includes family and friends who can help be supportive. This guide was written for people who are willing to work towards the goal of helping someone they care about learn new and healthier ways of coping with living.

Why do written work and talk about it therapy? Journaling is a part of the therapy process. And, when used to augment therapy, it can be a powerful and helpful tool. These exercises were designed to provide structured interactions, hopefully in a contained and directed manner. This journal is to give therapists working with families and people with deliberate self-destructive impulses, urges and behaviors a structured way to work on *one important lesson at a time*.

In my experience working with people who self-injure, I learned from watching the struggles, what they find helpful and not helpful. A number of these journaling assignments were developed while working with families working towards the goal of learning to think in differently way about a difficult set of problems, influencing their family life and relationships.

One lesson I want to emphasize is the *language* in this journal. It is deliberate. I get feedback that sometimes that the language is somewhat formal and the constructs are complicated. This is probably true. I think my patients are an intelligent group of people, and I adjust my language to help the individual master the constructs. It is, in my opinion, my job to work through, and teach the patient the language. *It is our job as clinicians to not just photocopy written exercises and tell our patients to do them.* When we discuss the materials on these pages, we are teaching them:

- Language skills for communication and expression.
- How to interact, get their needs met appropriately.
- How to tolerate frustration.
- How to tolerate having to ask for help appropriately.
- How to tolerate getting helped.
- How to tolerate interaction and closeness.
- How to ask questions and think about things, and then sit with them.
- It is an opportunity to have healthy mentoring interactions which help with attachment, modeling and social skills.
- It is an opportunity to build off of their existing skills, intelligence and resources.

- It is a teaching opportunity!

There are many components needing to be addressed in treatment. These include creating a working agreement, healthy limits and boundaries, structure and accountability. Much of what we clinicians do, to a great degree, is healthy parenting and helping to develop healthy attachments, age-appropriate skills development and maturity. Expecting that someone can self-manage is an important belief, and it is reasonable to believe this growth is going to be difficult. Many of our patients don't understand that their feelings are *reasonable*, and serve as data that something important is going on. Feelings aren't facts though, and it is important *to think reasonably* through our problems. It is our job to help them learn these lessons.

This work is based on the theoretical concepts of self-management and learning to tolerate and manage reactions to feelings. There are many influences to this approach to self-regulation, most specifically of structural process model developed by John Levitt, Ph.D. (2004); other influences come from cognitive behavior, family systems, object relations, mind/body approaches and developmental theories.

This work is not designed to emphasize memory-based recovery work. The focus in these activities is learning to manage the effects of the past in the present here and now. It involves being alive and grounded in the present and creating a new future, using the past as a frame of reference only. In our philosophy, the focus on traumatic memory work when someone can't manage the day to day life may be overwhelming, and cause trauma in the present. *There is a time and a place for that work: after safety, security and physical well-being are established.*

Therapy with Someone Who Self-Injures

There are cases and problems that tend to cause therapists to step back and think twice about engaging in a therapeutic relationship. These tend to be centered on high risk, suicidal, impulsive and /or destructive problems. The following section is designed to address a number of issues to help therapists have a different perspective on managing these types of problems within a therapeutic setting and relationship. This section is written strictly from the perspective of my own training and experiences.

When I supervise or consult, I use a few foundation considerations as *my* points of reference:

POSITION:

- There is no negotiation with or about Safety, Security and Physical Well-Being.
- Decisions are made on EVIDENCE or DATA, not intentions or effort.
- Structure has to be at the level the patient/family is functioning.
- Therapy is not PERSONAL to me. The presenting problems are not mine; therefore, there is no reason to respond personally as if the person is being defiant, oppositional or resistant. Asking, "how do you want me to respond to that?" is a great modeling question. It demonstrates that I can choose how to respond/react; and it allows them the opportunity to tell you what they want. You can then respond reasonably and appropriately.
- People don't have to "prove" anything to me. This is especially true about trust. Saying to them "Why should I believe you?" puts us both into a power struggle, where they will lose face. Saying "What is the evidence that your words and behaviors will be congruent?" is far more accurate. Ok, translate that to people-speak; "How do you know you will be safe?" "How will you know if you are becoming overwhelmed?"
- Don't try to cover too much ground at one time. Stick to one topic/issue and cover it in depth.
- If people can't keep themselves safe, it isn't time to be talking about memories of trauma. Timing is everything.
- My role as the therapist is:
  - Guide/teacher of the process
  - Be the "holder" of:
    - Expectations
    - Accountability
    - Containment
    - Structure
    - Pacing, timing and intensity
  - Be the "reminder" of:
    - What is the desired outcome or goal
    - Values guiding the decision making process
    - Options to achieve the desired goal or outcome
    - Opportunities to try something new occur every moment
    - They are going to need to try something new pretty often

- What the consequences or outcomes are for the decision options
- Rules, obligations and expectations
- Responsibilities appropriate to age and developmental capacities
- Healthy relationships
- What is "reasonable" and "unreasonable"
- Pointing out the obvious inconsistencies and incongruities and the outcomes, and asking if the "WHEN…THEN…" connections are what is desirable.
- Being direct, honest and containment
  - Interact based on the expectation that the individual can manage their own life without self-injury or other self-destructive behaviors.

LANGUAGE & TALKING:
- Language is important. Clarifying *meaning* is a critical aspect of teaching language and conceptualization for expression and skill attainment.
- Asking *how* they understand what is being said is important. "What did you hear me say?" is a great question.
- Break things down, don't talk AT them.

RECOGNIZE THE PHYSICAL CUES:
- Interrupt escalation of affect or confusion (overwhelm) with physical interruptions.
- Stand up, breathe, use the grounding exercises to interrupt physical escalation.
- Reflect to them the observations you see. "May I tell you what I am seeing?" "Are you aware that your body is…."
- CONNECT mind and body through stretching, breathing, and moving.
- Teach physical state awareness and connection.
- Connecting parasympathetic (relaxation) skills to stimulation (sympathetic) is important. You can't be both simultaneously.

CHOICE & PERSONAL RESPONSIBILITY:
- People do not have to choose to be healthy. They can un-choose it and decide to be unhealthy. The therapists' obligation is to then decide to move the person to the next level of care, or to un-choose working with the patient.
- The goal of therapy is to help the person become able to THINK their way through their life (real and perceived demands, problems, situations) and to make decisions based on THEIR BEST INTERESTS (which is managing one's Safety, Security and Physical Well-Being appropriately for their age and developmental level).
- Avoid power struggles. No one ever wins a power struggle, and no one wants to be a loser. Therefore people, when pushed into a battle, will often make choices to "win" over losing. Every one must have the option of saving face.
- The person, as a result of their choices and actions, "earns" or comes into a set of consequences. Let's define that word. Consequences are costs/benefits or outcomes of behaviors. They can be desirable or undesirable. They can be logical or natural outcomes. You, the therapist, do not experience the consequence. Your obligation is to have stated, known expectations and limits, and discuss them and the plan of action if needed. This is your containment and stated parameter.
- Because I, the therapist, do not experience the consequence, and the problem is not mine, I can remain neutral and act as a guide/teacher to the person, at least until the

parameters of safety and physical well-being are compromised and I act according to these known parameters.

How therapy is about age & developmental functioning, and to some extent, parenting.

It is important to model those skill sets we expect our patients and their families (or those involved in the process with them). And, part of doing this also involves teaching as we go. If you parallel process how we teach small children skills to the therapy process, it becomes much clearer and simpler. By this, I mean, when we teach children skills, we talk very concretely to them through challenges. We are often encouraging of them; encouraging them to problem solve it, and praising their efforts at trying and at achieving. We verify their comprehension of what we are saying or doing. We show them and then ask them to show us how they do it. It is always a good sign when you observe a child talking to him or herself and working their way through mastering something, and then to own that they did it themselves. This mastery is the foundation of age and developmentally appropriate self-regulation.

Unfortunately, as children become older and more verbal, we, as parents or therapists, tend to change our expectations and move away from this strategy. As therapists, we assume their expressive language reflects their ability to manage affect-laden thoughts, impulses and intensity. When we shift to being less structured and assume that they can manage without regard to the actual evidence, it can be a set up for the person. People, regardless of their age, need structure at the level where they are functioning, and to be held accountable for *reasonable* behavior within age and developmental parameters.

It is important to talk about the goals of treatment. Specifically, discuss whether or not the goal that the person is willing to develop a range of healthy skills to help them manage their safety and well-being. This discussion can clarify their level of preparedness to change and to clarify that they cannot be safe, healthy, and self-destructive at the same time. While we cannot mandate abstinence from self-destructive behaviors, we can indicate that there are reasonable limits to working with someone who is unwilling to commit to a goal of being safe.

As a therapist, you need to be prepared to have people opt to leave therapy, and to tell you they aren't willing to be safe and adhere to a therapeutic contract. If they need to be in a higher level of care, then so be it. You may need to face the fact that they can leave treatment. You also can set the parameters about how you will remain in the therapeutic relationship. You need to verbalize this and stand by it. Not in a threatening manner, but in a way that models reasonable and responsible management of relationships. I don't negotiate safety, and I don't negotiate the parameters of remaining in a relationship where the individual chooses to be unhealthy, dishonest and unwilling to follow the agreed upon parameters.

EVERY interaction with a patient and family is a THERAPEUTIC one.

Every interaction with other staff members is an opportunity to build relationships and support network, making the structure we use to contain the milieu stronger.

Every word, action and behavior by you with another person is a teaching opportunity.

Important concepts to keep in mind and to base your interventions on:
1. The goal is to help the individual self-regulate or self-manage.
2. The goal is to model self-regulation and management in EVERY interaction.
3. Emphasizing behaviors that help move the person towards their desired outcome.
4. Emphasizing problem-solving to tolerate affect and delay of gratification.
5. Containment. We operate on a framework of self-management. It isn't just about the identified patient; we have to model it too.
6. Use of the every conversation is an opportunity to provide for support and feedback.
7. Every action and word needs to be about self-regulating and containment, of the unit, program, patient/family and OURSELVES.

How do we do this?
1. Goal setting is one way to ground the individual in the focus of all activity.
2. Goal review is the feedback and reality testing to gather data about focus, behavior and accuracy of effort.
3. Redirect and discuss how they can make positive use of the group.
4. Emphasize reliance on problem-solving strategies, i.e., "what are you willing to try to work through this problem?"
5. Emphasize using the group or family process to ask for feedback and support.
6. Tolerating affect or "sitting with the feelings" while they "try something new," or goal directed behavior.
7. As a treatment provider representing a treatment philosophy, we need to operate with the same principles and structure, and our interventions need to be consistent.
8. As a treatment provider representing a treatment philosophy, we need to be contained, managing our own stress and feelings appropriately.
9. As a treatment provider representing a treatment philosophy, our interventions need to be about the patient attaining self-regulation and management. Even casual comments can undo your therapeutic efforts.
10. As a treatment provider, we need to present as a unified structured system (like a family), and think along the lines of inclusion and support of one another. A staff member from a different level of care is an extension of the treatment team, and you are important supports for one another. Include them and welcome them when they come on to your unit or into your program. Often they can provide critical pieces of information and assistance in transition for the patient. We are here because of the patient.

Translating into "Real Family Life" Experience

Talking with families about *reasonable* expectations and accountability is a critical first step in treatment. Asking a family what their values are and how they demonstrate it in their daily lives is a critical foundation issue for families. Often the answer I hear is that they are "too busy" or that they never thought about it. This is like taking off on a sailboat into open water without knowing how to sail, where you are going, or what you need and then being surprised when they get lost, take on water or get into trouble when the sea gets rough.

Further, as children become older and more verbal, we also provide more negative feedback, especially if their behavior displeases or inconveniences us. As therapists, it is neither helpful to them to be overly praising or to be punitive. Our emotional tone is neutral, looking at the evidence or data of the situation. Our role is to be a teacher of skills and to allow them to think their way through alternatives. Further, it is helpful to ask them if they desire/prefer the outcome of their choices. This is the "IF ....., THEN...." sequence. Working through this and allowing them to see the cause-effect of their challenges is part of helping them developmentally move to become more self-regulating and self-efficacious.

As the child gains more verbal ability, our structure changes and we begin to reward them, without attachment to the actual skill level and self-management capacities. So often they don't connect increased appropriate responsibility and self-management to increased freedoms and privileges. Consequently, many kids become very entitled, "I deserve it," without it being connected to the concept of investment in earning it through demonstrating reasonably consistent self-management and investment in the family. This is a critical concept for families to address in therapy. Often the family wants to be "good" or "kind" at the expense of teaching a child a lesson in self-regulation and reasonable expectations for appropriate behavior.

The parents may be quick at restricting them from their cell phones, computers, privileges, etc., but this is at the cost of the lesson. The lesson should be that privileges are earned as a result of first and foremost, consistent demonstration that the child is able to keep themselves safe and healthy. The other critical concept here is that these kids often have too much freedom and privilege and they need structure, clearly stated rules and expectations and to be held accountable BEFORE they are given the material privileges and privileges they can't emotionally handle.

So our conversations with our children are often interactions where they have most of the language skills, but not much in the way of true life experience and understanding of concepts is limited to their age and life experience.

We, as parents and as therapists, often TALK TOO MUCH. We talk until we think/feel they understand us. What happens is that they stop listening, generally because they are so flooded with affect and internal intensity. This provokes some of the shutting down, and some of the "urge" to injure to drive down internal intensity. Remember, it is pretty typical of adolescents to experience when they are being talked to and they are being challenged, to describe this as "being yelled at" and they don't listen. At this point the power struggle to save face and "win" the battle becomes the goal.

What is Self-Destructive Behavior and Thinking?

Definition

This behavior is called many names, including self-injury, cutting, self-mutilation and para-suicide. Most recently, it has been termed Nonsuicidal self-injury or NSSI. One definition is, "the intentional destruction of body tissue without suicidal intent and for purposes not socially sanctioned" (Klonsky & Muehlenkamp, 2007). This means that the person purposefully harms their own body without intending to die, and that this behavior is not socially sanctioned, such as piercing or tattooing.

Self-injurious behavior also includes to *thinking*. This is a set of behaviors, thinking and feelings. This is where *intention* comes into consideration. Our thoughts are tied to our behaviors, reactions and feelings. Often when the person changes their behavior, the thoughts and feelings remain unchanged. This is something that therapists want you to understand: *self-destructive behavior is only part of the problem, and is only part of what will need to change.*

Please don't call them by their behaviors, that is, "cutter." Once an identity is formed around such a label, it is hard to change self-definition. It removes the idea that there is ability to control or change behavior.

Self-Destructive Behaviors and Thoughts

Nonsuicidal self-injury can include any number of behaviors or patterns of behaviors, including ritual self-harm. These behaviors can include cutting, burning, scratching, carving, and insertion of objects under the skin. It can also include eating, drinking or swallowing non-food items. There can also be high-risk behaviors such as starvation, drug use, jumping out of moving cars, sexual activities and fighting.

Along with these behaviors are negative and self-destructive thoughts. It is important to understand that our *thinking colors the way we see and respond to the world.* It isn't always accurate or realistic. In addition, our body responds to our thoughts. If you've ever had the experience of being very angry, think about the state of your body. You probably were tense and ready to battle. Over time, the body becomes very able to respond in a way the mind and feelings don't know yet.

Some people have complicated rituals of injury. Sometimes people will go from one type of self-harming behavior to another, such as restricting, binging and throwing up, to cutting, to drug use and sexual acting out.

Sometimes people will pull their eyelashes or hair out compulsively. If this is the only type of self-harm seen, it is important to consider that this may be a form of obsessive-compulsive behavior. If this is the case, then evaluation with someone who specializes in this type of problem is highly recommended.

In some cases, people will also be highly anxious, refuse to go to school or are afraid of school. Their self-injury may help them manage these fears. Again, if this is the case, then evaluation with someone who specializes in this type of problem is highly recommended. Avoidance of school or leaving the home is never recommended, as it may reward the avoidance and fear and actually make it worse.

It is also common to see all sorts of eating disordered behaviors in someone who uses self-injury. Treating both problems is important. The same goes for substance abuse. If the therapist treating your loved one suggests treatment for these problems, listen to them and follow their recommendations. These behaviors are used to help manage feelings and are unhealthy *patterns* of behavior, they all are used to help manage, but not in a healthy way.

Who Self-Injures?
Depending which study you read, between 13.9% (Ross et al., 2008) of people in the community, up to 50% of teenagers and 35% of college students have admitted they have injured themselves (Gratz, 2001; Lloyd-Richardson et al., 2007; Nock et al., 2007, Whitlock et al., 2006). Even once people seek therapy, many people don't tell their therapist about the behaviors. In a study of college students, only 21% ever talked about to a counselor (Whitlock, Eckenrode & Silverman, 2006). This highlights the importance of asking about the self-injurious behavior and thinking directly.

Why?...or a better question, HOW is it helpful?
It is hard to think about self-destructive behaviors and thinking can be *helpful* to the person. The behavior has a PURPOSE in that it helps the person manage. It can help the person manage their feelings and thought, or as they will tell you, how it feels "inside" their body and head. So it can help them feel alive (increasing the ability to think and feel), or help them numb it (quieting or decreasing the intensity) (Brown, Comtois, & Linehan, 2002; Nock & Kessler, 2006; Suyemoto, 1998). Another reason is to release tension (Andover, Pepper, Ryabchenko, Orrico, & Gibb, 2005). Some studies have reported that this can help them stop bad feelings, feel alive, and to communicate with other people (Nock & Kessler, 2006).

Simply put, self-destructive behaviors can be thought of serving at least one of four functions (Nock & Cha, 2009):
- To generate feelings, usually from a very numb or empty state
- To escape or lessen bad or negative feelings or thoughts
- To get attention or something from other people or relationships
- To avoid or escape from demands

It is important to make a statement about *seeking attention*. Remember that it is a good thing when people we care about want our attention. This is a very easy thing to address. If someone is so wanting of your attention, think about ways to help this happen. If someone is using self-injury to get your attention, the worse thing you can do is punish them. It is reasonable to expect that people want your attention, but if they want your attention, *they need to use appropriate ways of getting it*. That being said, you must be open to giving them positive attention for positive and age-appropriate behaviors.

Many people immediately think that something terrible must have happened to make someone do this behavior. Actually, that tends not to be true for most people. It is a good question to ask. However, there is a bigger issue. Family conflict and fighting with parents is a common reason given for younger adolescents, and problems with close friends and girl/boyfriends for older adolescents and young adults (Hurry, 2000). The person may not have the ability or maturity to manage these relationships, so understanding both the persons' ability and the influence of the health in both family and social relationships is important. Social skills may not develop evenly. People who self-injure may show some skills in some areas, and not in others, and feel less able to handle situations and problems (Nock & Mendes, 2008).

Lastly, childhood neglect and abuse, family conflict and parental mental health are factors that need to be understood. These cause problems with healthy development and learning skills to manage in relationships in age-appropriate and socially appropriate ways. Learning how to live in the world begins at home. Every person living in the child's home teaches the child something about how to live in the world. Parental health and mental health are significant factors contributing to a child's well-being (Chitsaebesan, Harrington, Harrington & Tomenson, 2003). Children are great observers, and often do not know what they are seeing, but they are learning the rules of life from watching their families and the people in their lives.

How it is different from suicide
It is important to understand that the person may be suicidal or have suicidal thoughts, but the purpose of the behavior is TO STAY ALIVE. Self-injury behavior and thinking is a paradoxical behavior, it is used to stay alive. The goal of suicide is to die.

People who self-injure tend to have problems with managing the real and perceived demands of daily living, even if they are doing well in one or more areas. Even if they can problem solve and manage some social situations, they may not be able to manage everyone equally as well. This means the person may be a great student, but injure to manage their feeling that everyone believes they have to be perfect. They probably need professional support even if they say they can control it, or "it happened only once" or it is just a minor injury. In one study, they found that almost 25% of people who have injured will be seen again by medical professionals for injuring within a year; and about 4% of die by suicide within 5-10 years (Beenewith, Stocks, Gunnell, Peters, Evans & Sharp, 2002).

While it is hard to understand, these behaviors and thoughts help people stay alive and manage their feelings and relationships. Current studies suggest that more than half (52.9%) reported they use the behavior to "stop bad feelings" and not to die (Nock & Kessler, 2006). Further studies have shown that suicidal individuals who self-injure typically make suicide attempts during periods of time when they are not using self-injury to manage (Gratz, 2006). It is important to understand what the purpose of the behavior is to the purpose. *"How is it helpful?"* is a much more useful question than *"why did you do it?"*

Are there other problems too?

It is very common that someone who engages in self-injury also has other mental health problems. One study suggested that up to 99% of people who self-injure have some kind of mental health problem (Isacsson & Rich, 2001). In studies looking at teens in an inpatient hospital setting, 61% have a history of self-injury (Nock & Prinstein, 2004). The most common problems appear to be anxiety, depression, post-traumatic stress, eating disorders, substance abuse, anger management, problems with authority, antisocial behaviors, poor self-esteem and impulsivity (Isacsson & Rich, 2001; Jacobsen & Gould, 2007; Nock , Holmberg, Photos & Michel, 2007).

About changing the behavior and thinking patterns

This pattern of thinking, feeling and acting is very difficult to change. This is especially true if the person has been using self-injury to cope for a very long time, or if the person has been using a set of behaviors, like eating disorders, cutting, drugs and sex.

One of the first steps in changing the behavior pattern is the understanding that it serves a purpose to the person (Nock & Prinstein, 2004, 2005; Suyemoto, 1998). This is difficult to accept, especially if you don't understand it. The goal is to help the person develop other healthier ways to manage coping, problem-solving and living their life. This involves "sitting-through" feelings and not acting on them. It also involves willingness to try new things, and create new patterns of behavior, even when the immediate outcome doesn't make the person feel immediately "better." Learning to think through the problem instead of reacting emotionally is important. Likewise, learning a new language and set of skills to communicate thoughts and feelings is important.

What you can do to help…

Read this handbook and serious think about the information that is presented here. Most people are honestly trying to do the best they can, and would never intentionally try to hurt another person. If you are one of the people, please read this book as helping build off those good intentions.

Recovery involves addressing the mind, the body, the environment and relationships. This book is not written to criticize, judge or shame anyone. People are complicated, and relationships are complicated. Please read these pages as offering you something new to think about and offering you a new way to think about your relationship. At this point parents often think about how inconvenient change is, and that their routine "works" for their family. This is an opportunity to review just how healthy the family is, and whether or not the convenience and patterns cause health to be neglected. If your kid can't find health in your home, where will they ever learn it?

Lastly, understand that there may need to be some serious changes in your home, with how you and your family live with and relate to each other. Anyone living in the home influences any other person there. If you are an adult living in a home with a child, whether you are the parent or not, you are a role model to that child. There may need to be some very difficult changes made about household rules, responsibilities and privileges. Children and teens often know more than they let on. If you as adult isn't healthy, you are modeling your behavior. You change your behavior, the course of the health in your home changes too. Look for opportunities to teach through your actions and your words (this is called congruence).

If you are a teenage or young adult living in a house with someone who isn't healthy, you may need to figure out how to be healthy and keep yourself safe until you can be on your own. This is a very sad situation that does happen. You can love people and still be sad and disappointed; this is something to grieve through. Destroying yourself because of what someone did to you, or because someone can't or won't be who you need them to be, is not the answer. You may need to change how you relate to them, and accept what they can and can not be for you.

If the treatment team has suggested medication, think about it, ask about it, and do research about it. Get a second opinion. Many of these problems have a biological basis. Would you try to treat cancer or diabetes "naturally"? Would you try to correct your blurry vision or headaches "naturally" if they interfered with your life? The medications might be helpful to assist in the therapy process. Medication may help make the biology of the body work better, helping you be better able to sleep, and regulate your body functioning. You should make an informed decision. Taking medication is not a weakness. Is wearing glasses or a hearing aid weak? However, if medication is used, it is not a cure-all to the problem; this is a life-style change as well.

People often neglect the importance of the biology and healthy body functioning. It is important that people who are trying to be healthy have a healthy diet, healthy eating patterns, and sleeping schedule. This regulates the body we live in and need to operate in our world. In our busy lives, we tend to ignore this and instead do what is convenient. Many of us don't think about or nutrition at all, eating what we prefer or is convenient. We allow our children to stay up on their computers and phones. These are the easiest to fix. Healthy routines allow our bodies to recover and become healthy.

Adults living in a home with a child or teen who self-injure have a great opportunity to help change the life of this person. Likewise, they can bring terrible pain and suffering. If you are an adult reading this because you care about someone who self-injures, please understand your own behavior and live your life speaks volumes more than your words. So if you, the adult in the home abuses substances, has an eating disorder, is involved in an abusive relationship, self-injures or has anger management problems, your efforts at changing your patterns will be a first step in bringing the entire family/household into a healthier balance. Children have a good awareness of their parents' problems and short-comings. They can tell you very often what they need from their parents, and what their parents can't or won't provide for them. The bottom line is that children need the adults living in their home to behave like responsible, mature adults who set limits, have expectations and provide consistency, feedback and nurturance.

Being a parent is not easy. Practicing and modeling the behavior you want them to demonstrate, and being consistent is necessary. Look for opportunities to be a responsible parent, teaching lessons about how to manage in this world. While their (mis)behavior may be inappropriate or unacceptable, and you don't have to accept it, be prepared for how you are going to handle it when this occurs. That is why having known and predictable limits, expectations, outcomes (consequences), all predicated on family values.

Another critically important thing is to have limits, expectations, and clear accountability in your relationships. There is more about this later in this book. The message is that to be healthy, one needs to be involved in healthy relationships. Healthy relationships have rules, expectations, limits, and boundaries. They also have rules and, to some extent, a hierarchy. These are based on age and developmentally-appropriate standards. One problem with teens who self-injure, is that far too often, they have many more privileges than they have the emotional maturity to manage.

It is important that they know what is and what is not acceptable behavior, and when they chose unacceptable behavior, that is showing you that they are unable or unwilling to keep themselves safe, and you then structure them at that level. In addition, they have little understanding of responsibility, and expect that they can have what they want with little effort. Parenting is about working from the framework at where the person is showing they can or will manage, and providing only the privileges and freedoms that they can safely and consistently manage. If they want more freedom, less structure and privilege, your job as a parent is to allow them to earn it over time. If your 8-year-old is acting like a 4-year-old, you don't give them privileges and freedoms of an 8-year-old, you structure them like a 4 or 5 year-old until their behavior changes. This is an extremely important concept for people who are self-destructive: if your 16-year-old is acting like an 11-year-old and is unwilling or unable to keep herself safe and healthy, why are you letting her drive, be out of the house at parties, date older boys, be on her computer without you supervising her and why are you treating her like she is 21 or older (taking her shopping, getting her hair done, nails done, letting her smoke and drink and condoning her being sexually active with these older boys)? When you do this, you send a mixed message, and teach her she can behave however she wants, and there will be fights, but she can do what she wants. You end up looking, and feeling, like the one out of control.

One comment about the terms *age-appropriate* and *developmentally appropriate*, as these are important to growing up able to cope with life. There are certain lessons that have be learned at certain times in life, otherwise, the brain doesn't master these lessons well, causing problems further down the road. Some of these lessons is learning how to live with rules within a group of people and appropriate expression and managing of emotions. If you are a parent who believes that your child doesn't need rules and limits, because they are a child/teen, and that they can learn these later, you are setting your child up for problems later in their lives. If they don't grow up with limits, values, and expectations, they miss learning how to live and function appropriately in society. It is hard to hold down a job, have healthy relationships and live independently if they have never learned these lessons at home. Think about it, if your child behaved at school or work the way they behave at home, would that be acceptable? It is important that they learn these lessons at home. Believe it or not, their brain is forming daily, and each interaction they have impacts brain development, maturity, and coping ability. This is especially important for self-management, development of self-definition, expression and management of emotions.

Understand that people who are giving up a pattern of self-injury struggle, and often feel worse before they get better. Often when they feel worse (meaning they are experiencing thoughts and emotions without automatically acting out), they are more expressive (yelling, crying, sulking). This is tough to live with at home, but considering the alternative of self-destructive behaviors, this is far more developmentally appropriate. Your job in this case is to set limits on what is appropriate or acceptable for expression and behavior in your home.

That is why therapy and support can be so helpful; it gets everyone through the tough times. Sometimes, the behavior relapses, and that does not mean the person failed or that therapy failed. These are opportunities to talk about what was working, where the struggle was, and why self-injury seemed like the "right answer." It is important that people keep their therapy appointments, and if the patient won't go, the parent should go and talk to the therapist and figure out how to handle this power struggle appropriately. This is something to talk about *with the therapist*.

This part of the book focuses on parenting, rules, communication, roles and boundaries. Why talk about this in a book about self-injury? There are several reasons:

- The family relationship is the main relationship, where the person lives, learns about and practices the way relationships work.
- The goal of parenting a healthy child is to raise a child who can be self-sufficient and who is able to function in the world in a positive way. The goal of therapy is pretty much to help this happen, although the relationship is different.
- The goal of parenting a healthy child is to parent towards what a child needs, not what is convenient for the parent, or based on what a child wants. In this case, because of the self-destructive behaviors, what a child needs and fostering health is most important.
- Therapy works based on reasonable and age and developmentally appropriate rules, expectations, accountability, and limits. These are the foundation for recovery, and they become the road map when someone is struggling.
- Therapists and parents have similar, although someone different, roles and responsibilities. Teaching parents about the foundation of structure and support is part of helping the person be able to practice new behaviors.
- Parental mental health is one of the best predictors of a child's well-being and absence of self-destructive behaviors (Chitsabesan et al., 2003).

Activity: Parenting Styles and Goals

How do you describe your parenting style and goals? How well are they working for you and your children?

Do people living in your home know these goals and ideas and why you think they are important?

Activity: Defining Health for Your Family

How do you define "health" for people in your family?

In what ways does your family structure help people be healthy?

What do you want to teach your children about health? How can you do this?

Do you have rules about nutrition, sleep and self-care? Do these help people in your family take care of health?

Are there ways that you might consider need change to help people be healthy?

What does a _healthy_ family need to be healthy?

Age appropriate and developmentally appropriate:

- Values = principles, morals, standards
  - That are based on age and developmentally appropriate standards
  - That are based in family practices
  - What are the values you want to teach your children? How do demonstrate those to your children? Do the children know what are important character values?
  - Understanding that health is important
  - In healthy families, their words and their practices are similar. This is called congruency. They say that health is important, so there are practices that assure people are eating a balanced diet, having an appropriate sleep schedule, and reasonable amount of physical activities.
- Rules = Guidelines, standards, operating system
  - There are reasonable rules about behaviors and expectations
- Expectations = Belief, anticipated outcome
  - That people will behave with respect, demonstrate healthy behavior
  - That there are known rules and expectations for behaviors, and when these are meet this is considered as positive and mature; and when not met there are reasonable and known consequences.
  - That people will uphold the family values
- Roles = Function, responsibility, job, task
  - Adults are adults, teens are teens, children are kids
  - People are responsible for behaving responsibly and maturely
  - Adults model the behavior they want to see in the children/teens
- Accountability = Responsibility, what you answer for, standard you are responsible for meeting
  - They are responsible for their words and actions
  - Everyone is responsible for upholding the family values
- Responsibility to the family
  - They owe the family some form of respect, helping the household work
  - Their behavior is appropriate
- Hierarchy = Chain of command, responsibility & structure order
  - Parents and adults in the house are responsible for overseeing the household structure, and holding people accountable to the family structure, and provide the consequences for behavior
  - The adults are adults and behave as such
- Purpose = Reason, aim, goal, target
  - What is the purpose of Family? What does your family stand for, why have a family, what did you want? What do you want to create?
  - What do you stand for as a family? How do you create that?
- Rights/privileges = Those benefits earned or given
  - Are the rights and privileges age-appropriate?
  - Are people able to handle the rights and privileges they have? Does their behavior reflect appropriate emotional and behavioral maturity?
  - Do they have value and meaning to the person? Are they earned or given?

- Responsibilities/Obligation = Duty, task, ownership, charge
  - Do people in your family understand responsibility to the family and feel an obligation to being healthy for it?
  - Reasonable consequences (both positive and negative) = Result, outcome, effect
  - Are there opportunities to demonstrate that they can manage themselves in a healthy way consistently? Are there chances to earn positive attention?
  - Are the consequences reasonable when there are poor choices and unacceptable behavior?
- Stated values, belief system = Conviction, faith, principle, guidelines for living
  - Do your kids know what is important to your family?
  - Family rules and guidelines
- Investment in the family unit = Placing value and investing in the family unit
  - Everyone living in the family home contributes to the family unit in some way
  - Attachment, belongingness, support
  - Family times designated
  - Eat together, the more often, the better. Have expectations of healthy meals, people helping out and participating appropriately.
  - Everyone contributes to the well-being and running of the house
  - Does everyone in the household uphold these definitions?

Because there is someone who engages in self-injury, the need for these to be talked about and openly known is even more important. In some ways, by practicing these as mindfully as you used to practice tying shoes, brushing teeth, or saying "please" or "thank you", you help them learn:

- To plan and anticipate
- Especially the "if I……, then……..will happen"
- To tolerate frustration
- To problem-solve
- To delay gratification
- To cope
- Skills of daily living
- The importance of family
- The importance of family values as a framework and reference
- Logical and natural consequences for actions
- To demonstrate ability to make things right, earn trust and respect

A consequence is the "THEN" part of the IF…..THEN…….. equation.
Consequences can be positive, as well as negative. They are not the same as punishment.

Logical consequence = an logical outcome that happens as a consequence of an action
> Example: If you leave your room a mess and treat your possessions with disrespect, a LOGICAL consequence is that you are not allowed to use the family car and that we will not purchase you more items as you can't show those you own.

Natural consequence = a natural consequence that occurs as a result of an action
> Example: I didn't study for a test, I took poor notes, and didn't pay attention in class, and I failed.

Activity: Values = Principles, Morals, Standards

Define ideas that you have about each of these:

- That are based on age and developmentally appropriate standards
- That are based in family practices
- What are the values you want to teach your children? How do demonstrate those to your children? Do the children know what are important character values?
- Understanding that health is important
- In healthy families, their words and their practices are similar. This is called congruency. They say that health is important, so there are practices that assure people are eating a balanced diet, having an appropriate sleep schedule, and reasonable amount of physical activities.

Values	How do you teach, live or practice this value?
Are there any that you have trouble practicing? Why is that?	

Stated values, belief system = Conviction, faith, principle, guidelines for living
- Organizing thoughts and values that anchor and guide the family
- Do your kids know what is important to your family?
- Family rules and guidelines are based on values and goals (hopes, aims)

Goals:
Part of recovery is making decisions about what is important. This is done by first defining what we want to accomplish by our efforts.

GOAL: Objective, aim, aspiration, target

Examples of goals include:
Being able to keep myself safe
Being able to problem-solve and manage my feelings and thoughts
Making decisions that help me be healthy

There are a couple of things to think about:
Don't make *not* goals, like "don't hurt myself"
Happiness is not a goal, it is a by-product of how we live our lives

---

Values:
Values are important to help guide our decisions and actions. Values help keep us on course when we are working towards something.

VALUE: principles, standards, worth, importance

In therapy, the goal is teach a person to make decisions in their own "best interests," which doesn't mean making decisions to make us happy, or necessarily to get what we want; but what is needed to be healthy.

It is important that families have values that are known and are something the entire family lives daily. Many times families don't practice.

Activity: Family Values Discussion

Discuss your family values. What are values are important to *each* member in your family?

As a whole family?

How do you teach these to your children?

VALUES

Values are necessary to help you have a healthy Framework to use in decision making. Values are something you can choose to adopt. They help you define who you are, and what you define as important to you. This foundation is necessary for guiding goals, your choices and actions:

Dignity	Self respect
Honesty	Telling the truth to others, honoring the truth
Integrity	Telling the truth to yourself, honoring your own truth
Respect	Having honor towards oneself and others
Responsibility	Having investment in owning what you commit to accomplishing
Accountability	Being willing to be responsible to commitments made
Willingness	Being open to trying new options or choices, motivation to be different
Openness	Being willing to be willing to try new options or choices
Tolerance	Being willing to put up with feeling or thoughts that are uncomfortable or new
Boundaries	Having healthy limits, respecting ones personal space
Patience	Endurance over a long period of time, keeping your eye on the future
Awareness	Having knowledge about experiences, reactions and thoughts
Mindfulness	Being aware of choices, reactions, and being present in the moment
Empathy	Having understanding and sympathy
Kindness	Being gentle and benevolent
Compassion	Having consideration, empathy and benevolence with another
Perseverance	Having determination and endurance towards something important
Cooperation	Aligning yourself with your goal and acting in your best interest

---

Activity: Identifying Your Values

Each person in the family: review these values. Which are important to you? For each one you pick how could you and your family put these into action and live them?

Rules = Guidelines, standards, operating system
Rules and expectations work best when they are connected to your family VALUES. List your values and an expectation or rule that is connected to that value.

- There are reasonable rules about behaviors and expectations

Expectations = Belief, anticipated outcome

- That people will behave with respect, demonstrate healthy behavior
- That there are known rules and expectations for behaviors, and when these are meet this is considered as positive and mature; and when not met there are reasonable and known consequences.
- That people will uphold the family values

Activity: Values and Expectations or Rules

Value	Expectation or rule
What are four rules that everyone in your family has to live by? In this family, we…	

Rules, continued
What are some additional expectations rules that you have related to what you expect
people in your family to live by? Think in terms of specific people, their ages, maturity
level and what they are able to do.

Activity: Expectations, Rules & How well is it working?

Expectation	Rules showing this	Is this working?

Are these rules working? Why or why not?

Activity: Roles & Hierarchy

Roles = Function, responsibility, job, task
- Adults are adults, teens are teens, children are kids
- People are responsible for behaving responsibly and maturely
- Adults model the behavior they want to see in the children/teens

Hierarchy = Chain of command, responsibility & structure order
- Parents and adults in the house are responsible for overseeing the household structure, and holding people accountable to the family structure, and provide the consequences for behavior
- The adults are adults and behave in age and role appropriate ways

Define the roles and responsibilities of the PARENTS or ADULTS in your home:

Define the roles and responsibilities of the children and teens in your home:

Do you talk about the difference between adults and children and the reason for this hierarchy?

Activity: Want Ad – Family Member

If you were to write a want ad for a parent (if you are a child), a child/teen (if you are a parent), spouse (if you are a spouse), what qualities would you ask for in that person? Go back to your list of values, and think about your responsibilities, values and goals for your home.

Wanted: A _____

In exchange, what could you offer?

Write about your feelings and thoughts about what you have versus what you hope to create.

Activity: Letter to Someone I Love

Sometimes when we are trying to be healthy, people and relationships in our lives aren't helpful. This can be a sad or painful fact, and make us angry and hurt. Sometimes we fear being alone so much that we stay in relationships that aren't good for us. We even put up with abuse, neglect and unhealthy rules. Sometimes we watch people self-destruct and feel helpless to help them.

Think about someone in your life right now. If you were thinking about what you need from them, what would you ask from them? What do you from them to be healthy? Can they give it to the relationship? What would the relationship need to be healthy?

Do you think they can be healthy? What would you do if they said no, or weren't able to?

Accountability = Responsibility, what you answer for, standard to meet
Responsibility to the family
- They owe the family some form of respect, contribution (i.e., helping the household work)
- Their behavior is appropriate for their age, developmental level, and skills
- People are responsible for their words and actions
- Everyone is responsible for upholding the family values

Activity: Standards, Rules and Accountability
What standards do you have rules for and how do you hold people accountable?

How do you hold people accountable for their responsibilities? What behaviors do you check on and hold people accountable for doing? What happens when they do and do not do their responsibilities?

Person	Responsibility Given	How you hold them accountable
In reviewing this, are there things that work? What doesn't work well?		

Activity: Telling You My Thoughts about Your Behavior

An important part of a healthy foundation in a healthy relationship is holding people accountable for their behavior. This should be done with the following values in mind: honesty, compassion, respect and responsibility. Write a letter about:

- What do you want in your life for your family and relationship?
- What isn't working anymore?
- Why do you want to change now?
- What do you want to know or say about the self-destructive behavior?
- What are you willing to do differently? What aren't you willing to do?

Activity: Understanding how do you impact other people?

It is important to look at how you impact the people in your life. Here's what you do: This week, pay attention to how people react to you. Even with your best intentions, how do you think your actions and behavior influence the different people in your life? In this exercise think about how your behavior, emotions, attitudes and reactions impact people. Is the reaction you get what you want? Are there outcomes that you would like to be different? Is there a particular person you may impact the most?

Write about the experience:

Activity: Understanding the Choices I Make

It is important to understand that you make choices about your behaviors. This is something that is difficult for many people to understand. Discuss about differences among each of you.

What are behaviors you use to help you stay alive and manage your feelings?

How are these behaviors helpful to you?

What kind of problems do you get into because of your self-destructive behaviors? How do they impact your relationships with other people?

Activity: What Would You Say?

I give myself very good advice, but I very seldom take it. Alice, Alice in Wonderland.

What would you say to your family if you could have them listen to you? Consider the people you live with, what are the important things you need to say. What is going on in your house and what do you need to fix it?

Dear...,

As you think about what you've written above, what is important that you say to your family?

What is working well? What do you like about your family life?

What is the biggest problem in your opinion?

Who can help and how?

What do you need to do to try to fix these problems?

If you share your letters with your family, make sure everyone listens and hears what concerns are being said. Respect the thoughts. THEN discuss what is REASONABLE, ACCEPTABLE and APPROPRIATE for your family as a unit. Everyone should have a say.

Rights/privileges = Those benefits earned or given
- Are the rights and privileges age-appropriate?
- Are people able to handle the rights and privileges they have? Does their behavior reflect appropriate emotional and behavioral maturity?
- Do they have value and meaning to the person? Are they earned or given?

Activity: Defining Rights & the Opportunity to Earn Privileges

List 10 rights that people in your family should have, and respect

List 10 ways people in your family can earn trust; respect and privileges (make a list for each person in your family):

Responsibilities/Obligation = Duty, task, ownership, charge
- Do people in your family understand responsibility to the family and feel an obligation to being healthy for it?

Reasonable consequences (both positive and negative) = Result, outcome, effect
- Are there opportunities to demonstrate that they can manage themselves in a healthy way consistently? Are there chances to earn positive attention?
- Are the consequences reasonable when there are poor choices and unacceptable behavior?

In order to have trust, respect and privileges, having responsibilities and obligations are necessary. These should be reviewed often, and changed as people grow, develop and change. There should also be opportunities for POSITIVE feedback, encouragement and earning trust, respect and privileges.

Activities: Responsibilities, earning trust, respect and privileges

Discuss as a family what are reasonable responsibilities to show how mature and responsible each of your children/teens.

Discuss as a family how someone can earn POSITIVE feedback, encouragement and earning trust, respect and privileges.

Specifically, what would you consider to be positive feedback? What words do you want to hear? Make a list from the parents' point of view and the person who self-injures perspective.

For the person who engages in self-injure: How will your family know you are behaving in a healthy way? What do you want feedback on?

What do you think is worthy of earning privileges? What privileges do you want to earn? (Each makes a list).

Investment in the family unit = Placing value and investing in the family unit
- Everyone living in the family home contributes to the family unit in some way
- Attachment, belongingness, support
- Family times designated
- Eat together, the more often, the better. Have expectations of healthy meals, people helping out and participating appropriately.
- Everyone contributes to the well-being and running of the house
- Does everyone in the household uphold these definitions?

Why the family and family structure is important
- The family is the first experience we have with relationships, rules of living, and how we take care of ourselves
- This is where we learn our foundation & rules for life, our framework for relationships with others and our own self-care
- This is where we learn about "bad" and "good", who to trust, lying, rules, breaking rules, what is important
- The family is the place where we learn life skills, like cooking, cleaning, laundry, etc. These practical skills are the foundation for learning how to be independent later in life, but also gives the person a way to contribute to the household
- Having a reasonable amount of responsibility for helping taking care of yourself and contributing to the household teaches the importance of the value of "In our family…"
- Observing how adults relate to each other and to their children
- When kids don't have chores or responsibility to the family,
- They don't learn important self-care skills and don't learn how to do important things that will help them become able to manage living independently
- They don't have the opportunity to learn about contributing to something bigger than them (the family unit), which is practice for having a job, and later having a family and being a parent
- They don't learn about responsibility and have opportunities to demonstrate that they are responsible and mature
- They learn that they get privileges without responsibilities or obligation
- The structure (rules, roles, expectations, rewards/consequences, responsibilities, feedback) and relationships are modeled, and this is where children learn about living and interacting with other people
- They learn about the rules for relationships and intimacy
- They learn about problem-solving, handling conflict and anger management
- Where we learn frustration tolerance
- Where we learn about expression of feelings and thoughts
- Where we learn what is acceptable or not acceptable behavior
- They learn about self-care, nutrition, and about health management
- They learn values, morals, develop belief systems
- *This is where we learn how to be people*, we grow through different stages and "practice" as we go!

- Think of these as teaching opportunities: opportunities to teach what you think is necessary and important about how to be healthy and able to cope in the world
- The person needs opportunities to practice
- Making mistakes and learning from them
- Doing well, behaving responsibly and appropriately, and demonstrating maturity and healthy self-management
- Developing healthy self-care skills
- Having healthy parent-child and sibling relationships
- Knowing what the expectations/consequences are and making decisions based on that
- Knowing and practicing the values, "in this family, we...."

Why the family and family structure is important for the person who self-injures
- The person who self-injures needs structure and feedback to help contain them.
- The person needs opportunities to practice managing in age and developmentally appropriate ways, and family structure provides this.
- The person needs opportunities to practice.
- Making mistakes and learning from them.
- Doing well, behaving responsibly and appropriately, and demonstrating maturity and healthy self-management.
- Developing healthy self-care skills.
- Having healthy parent-child and sibling relationships.
- Knowing what the expectations and consequences are and making decisions based on that
- Observing how adults relate to each other and to their children.
- Learning about roles and how they can be safe and mentoring.
- Learning about safety and how to keep themselves safe.
- Learning about tolerating authority, limits and expectations.
- By enforcing reasonable structure, limits and expectations, the person learns how to have healthy relationships and self-management.
- Learning and demonstrating efforts at healthy self-care.
- Learning that what they contribute is important to the family, and have a chance to matter in a positive way.
- Having a family unit based in values gives this person a foundation to make decisions based on known expectations and consequences.
- For example, if one of the family values is that people will be responsible for taking care of themselves and be healthy, the person knows that when they chose to self-injure, there will be a consequence for this action, such as having to be safe and without self-injury for a week before they are able to earn a privilege like being on the computer, driving the family car, or having their cell phone.
- Talk openly about what you want them to learn.
- Ask your child what they are learning from behaviors and the outcomes of their choices
- Ask them about what other choices that could have been made and what could have happened if they made other choices.
- Ask them about what they understand about their world.
- These are teaching moments!

Activity: In this family, we..........

In this exercise, work on these questions first individually, and then as a family. Compare your answers and listen to what each person has to say:

- Related to anger, in this family we

- Related to expressing feelings, in this family we

- Related to being able to express our thoughts or opinions, in this family we

- Related to being able to have different ideas or opinions, in this family we

- Related to being able to have something positive noticed about us, in this family we

- Related to drugs, alcohol, and other self-destructive behaviors, in this family we

- Related to healthy life styles, in this family we

- Related to being able to resolve conflict, in this family we

- Related to responsibilities, contributing to the family, in this family we

- Related to learning opportunities about important life skills, in this family we

- Related to healthy boundaries and roles (parents being parents, kids being kids), in this family we

- Related to respect, in this family we

- In this family, we belief the following things are important

- Related to what this family says is important, I

- Related to what this family says is important, we

- Related to earning respect and trust, in this family we

- Related to how well we can trust one another, in this family we

- In order to get attention in this family, we

- In order to get support, in this family we

- Related to the rules and values of this family, how well do we practice this?

What about family patterns?

Studies show that 50-75% of adolescents who self-injure will injure after arguments with parents (Hurry, 2000). With older adolescents and young adults, problems with close relationships are often sited as the reasons they injure.

It is important to look at:

- The rules of conflict and conflict resolution that are used in your family.
- The rules of relationships, how intimacy is handled, what is the foundation for healthy relationships.
- Conflict and conflict resolution teach some important life skills. It is important because they help teach respect, appropriate self-expression, how to handle conflict and resolve it. For children and teens, conflict with parents, when handled appropriately, teach skills like:
  - Respect for authority
  - Tolerance of frustration
  - Ability to tolerate and resolve conflict
  - Accepting outcomes
  - Reconciliation (making up, making things better)
- When you think about this, these are important skills that we all need to have relationships with others, and to be successful in a work or school environment. It is important that parents understand that having reasonable rules and tolerating only so much conflict before known consequences are earned, is important.

There are a number of different studies that suggest that eating and having time together as a family on a regular and expected basis builds and strengthens healthy children. Specifically, these children and teens:

- Are less likely to use drugs and alcohol.
- Are less likely to be involved in dangerous or high risk activities.
- Learn about how to take care of themselves.
- Have opportunities to practice language & communication skills.
- Have opportunities to talk with people who are important in their lives during a shared activity.
- Learn valuable self-care skills if they are included in meal planning, preparation, and clean up.
- Are more likely to be connected to their family in positive ways.
- Are more likely to respect family values and norms.
- Are more likely to have healthier nutrition and understanding of healthy eating and self-care patterns.
- Most experts suggest cooking only one meal, not different plates for everyone. This encourages people to try new foods and doesn't reward "picky" or "finicky" eaters, who may be emotionally in control of the family through their poor eating habits.
- If you want kids to be healthy, parents need to model healthy nutrition and decision making around self-care and eating.
- This is not the time to remind someone they are fat or to criticize weight.

- This is the time to remind people that nutrition is connected to making healthy choices about what their body needs in order to be healthy.
- It is reasonable to have structure, expectations and known consequences for behaviors. We all face them, whether we are grown-up or a child. What is a consequence? It is something that happens after a behavior. Known and consistent consequences help us learn the strategy of "if I do _____, then _____ is going to happen." Consequences are earned or given as a result of a behavior.
- Reasonable consequences and choices about behaviors are important to people. I can choose to behave in a certain way if I want something or if I want to avoid something. For example,
  - If I want to be able to use my parents' car, then I need to follow the rules and show my parents I am responsible enough to borrow it.
- If I drink and drive, then my parents will never let me borrow the car, and I'll be grounded for six months.

Too often parents give their children privileges without the child/teen:

- Being mature enough.
- Being able to socially and emotionally manage it.
- Being responsible.
- Having the maturity to manage it.
- Having earned it as a result of their ability to manage themselves.
- What happens often in our society is that children/teens are given privileges, and then when something happens, the parents punish them for it by removing the privileges. Significant conflict happens, mostly because the kid isn't mature enough to understand the link between their behavior and the consequences. They DON'T MAKE THE CONNECTION.
- This is especially true related to inappropriate and early sexualization of our children. We live in a society where children/teens are sexualized at younger ages, without maturity and social skills to manage these relationships. They aren't able to manage themselves well, and many times parents condone sexual behavior and social activities that these kids are not mature enough to handle.
- If your child, or you, is engaging in self-destructive behaviors, you may be lacking social and emotional skills to help you be healthy. *It is unreasonable to expect if you can't keep yourself safe, then you are not ready to move onto other demands of life.*
- Why would you allow a young girl who can't/won't eat enough to keep her body healthy, to go off to college, and walk to and from school three miles every day? Parents tell me they are supporting her dream of being a teacher, and walking "makes her happy." Parenting is about structuring our children to be healthy. Happiness is their own responsibility. This is simply supporting unrealistic self-appraisals, unhealthy and dangerous behaviors.
- Why would you take off every door in your home, not allow your daughter to shave her legs or be in the bathroom because you are afraid she is going to use a razor to cut herself or commit suicide, and yet give her the car to go out with her friends, and to drive her younger siblings around because you are busy? Happens every day.

Then the power struggles and screaming and fighting and threats and acting out happens. Parents usually given in, because the kid puts 100% energy into not losing and, face it, their whole world is tied up in this. Parents also give in because they become beaten down. In the process, they don't realize it, but they have just:

- Taught their kid that their bad behaviors, on top of the original inappropriate behavior, if kept up long enough, will defeat you. This is called bullying.
- Taught the kid that they don't have to be accountable for their inappropriate behavior. This is called irresponsibility and entitlement.
- Taught the kid that they can behave any way they want to get what they want without consequence or remorse. This is entitlement and anti-social behavior.
- Taught the kid that they don't have to manage their feelings or behaviors; that they can dump it on you, or hurt themselves, whatever they need to do so that they "win" or get their point across. This teaches immaturity and disregard for others.
- The bottom line is parents need to model and talk about healthy behaviors, conflict resolution, structure and values. This needs to be based on the emotional health and well-being of your child. It needs to include age-appropriate standards, expectations and opportunities to earn positive attention and rewards, and have consequences for poor choices too. However, if parents aren't modeling this, the child's chances are limited.
- Look for teaching moments with your child and family. What lessons do you want to teach your children about how to live in this world, and have a healthy and productive life?
- Parenting is hard and complicated. Seek support if you need it. Parenting children with special needs and problems may require ongoing help and mentoring.

In Summary

Consider your family and your family life as important to the health and well-being of everyone who lives there. Be honest about what you are willing to change and not change, and why. Look for teaching opportunities. *Instead of reacting out of your feelings, respond based your values, goals and what you want to teach your child.* Remember, everyday, you have a child who is older and more experienced, just as you had to change your patterns from when they went from infant to toddler, so the maturation and brain development continues! Some lessons are harder to learn if they are learned too late. Your child/teen is learning some of these lessons at a time when their brain was ready for it earlier, and now the window for learning those lessons has passed. That may be why in some ways your child/teen seems so mature and at the same time so unable to manage in other ways. These uneven developmental abilities benefit from structure, consistency and accountability. It is normal that they will fight that, and it is even more important that you parent

The home environment and relationships teach child how to live in the world and with other people. Your home is your child's first world. You can't wait for the world to teach your child how to survive in it. They are already learning from your home, from the adults and people in it. Your child/teen is learning even without you. If you are not structuring, setting limits and expectations on behavior, because you want your child to "be a kid" or "be happy," you are teaching them that rules for socially acceptable behaviors and self-management do not apply to them. What then happens is that they don't learn how to emotionally cope or problem-solve when they are frustrated, angry or manage. Your rules and the way you live teach the child/teen about the rules of living. Do your rules help your child/teen live in the world in a healthy way? Do your rules and practices in the home teach about balance, health and self-care? Do your relationships in your family teach about healthy communication, social skills, empathy and living with others?

Developmental changes do not necessarily mean that they have the right to behave inappropriately and that is where structure comes in. If you have someone in your family who is not healthy because of their self-destructive behavior and life style, it is a bigger problem. The good news is that if your family has a problem, then your family may be the key to helping resolve the problem!!

With some consideration to the way you think about your family life, and willingness to make health a priority, everyone wins! Your family can become calmer, more predictable, more connected, and in the long run, a much happier experience for everyone. If you have these as your intentions, you are off to a great start. Don't be afraid to ask for help and guidance, it will make you smarter and more confident in your choices.

One of the reasons that people engage in self-injury and self-destructive behaviors is for *communication*. Typically, people will try to lower the intensity of the feelings inside so they can think more clearly, or they will try to connect with people or express their feelings through self-injury.

These people often struggle with expressing their thoughts and feelings. This actually is very developmentally typical for most teens and children. So in some ways, the problem is typical, but their choice of management style is not. This is the easier problem to manage. Teaching language skills is a relatively easy thing to do.

Sometimes, the problem is bigger. Sometimes there is no one willing or able to listen to them, or to help them learn these skills. In some family systems, the pattern goes like this:
Person 1:   I think……
Person 2:   Well you should……………!
Person 1:   Whatever………! You never……………..
Person 2:   Don't speak to me like that!
Person 1:   Well you don't treat me with respect…..
And so on………….and no one ever talks about the real issue, everyone just gets angrier and angrier.

Healthy Communication Patterns
Healthy communication patterns are based on:
- The spoken message
- What is said verbally through words
- What is said through vocal tone, facial expression
- The received lesson
- What was heard
- How it was perceived and received
- The visual cues (facial, body language, personal space usage)

This involves:
- Listening to what is being
- Responding to what is being said
- Stating your position
- The MESSAGE said in WORDS
- The MESSAGE said in EMOTIONS
- The MESSAGE said in BODY LANGUAGE
- The MESSAGE said in VERBAL TONE

It also involves:
- Speaking and listening to the true message, and clarifying when you are uncertain.
- Being willing to interact from a thought-based not emotional framework.
- Managing your opinions.
- Being focused on the interaction in the moment.

- Paying attention to patterns in behaviors.
- Taking a WIN-WIN position, meaning that everyone needs to be heard, understood and be able to walk-away from the interaction having had their say, even if they didn't get their way.
- In other words, if you approach communication as a battle, there will be only a winner and a loser. Is that the message you want to teach your child? That they are a loser? That the only way to interact with others is through a string of wins and losses? That might makes right and it is about power?
- What are the opportunities in these interactions that you teach your child about self-expression, conflict resolution and management?
- Do not respond to emotion. Respond to logic.
- If this relationship is TRULY important to you, and teaching your child how to communicate in a healthy way, then you have to take the higher road. That means sticking to the structure and communicating through your stated values.
- Be willing to hear what is being said to you. Be willing to consider it.
- If you are talking about a set known structure, expectation, and the rules have been broken, let the consequence stand.
- This is a teaching moment. If they broke a rule, and you have a consequence, no matter how much they argue, posture, etc., you need to be the voice of logic and stand by your family rules.
- This teaches important lessons: tolerating frustrations, accountability for choices, and learning the language and skills to communicate maturely and appropriately.
- When you back down, or inconsistently apply rules and consequences, you send very mixed messages and basically teach your child how to bully, posture and have temper-tantrums to get their needs met.

Rules for Healthy Communication should include:
- Using "I" statements
    Example, "I am very angry...."
- Talking about specific behaviors
    Example, "....when you injured instead of talking to me."
- Talking about specific requests or demands logically (without emotion!)
    Example, "...In the future, I want you to think about talking to me before you injure because I want to be able to trust you."
- Labeling what you are willing to do to be helpful or what action you are willing to take if this situation happens again.
    Example, "If this situation happens again, and you don't ask for help and you decide to hurt yourself before you ask for help, then I will have to look at that behavior as demonstrating that you can't manage yourself and keep yourself safe. I will have to look at the Family Contract and see what reasonable structures should be put into place. Since this happened after you were online with your friends, I will think that not allowing you online, except to do your homework, until you can demonstrate you can make positive and healthy choices for at least two weeks."
- Acknowledge their feeling and the importance of their opinion to them.
    Example, "I understand you are angry, and this party is very important to you."
- Restate your goal & family value based position.

Example, "In this family, we have an agreement to make healthy choices, and you chose to make a self-destructive one. This shows that you are not mature enough to handle the privilege of going to a party and being without supervision."

In this family, we.........

This is an important statement that grounds you, the person with the overflowing and intense emotions, stay focused on what is important: Making decisions that are grounded in our family values.

Activity: Communication Rules

What are some rules for communication that you would like in your family? Example: People listen before responding

The family contract is written to help people with self-destructive behaviors know exactly what is expected of them and what the consequences, both positive and negative, are for the choices they make.

As parent(s) rules should be consistently enforced by all of the people involved in parenting the child and in each household the child lives.

Activity: Defining Expectations and Consequences

It is important to clarify what expectations you have in your family, and identify a list of reasonable consequences for them. This means both desirable and positive outcome as well as undesirable outcomes we want to avoid. A punishment is when something is taken away or something negative happens. Remember the goal of parenting is to encourage positive behavior, and allow the opportunity to gain something positive, and to have logical and natural consequences for behaviors. It is better to put someone in the position of being able to earn something positive, and then if necessary then take it away, and allow them the opportunity to earn it back.

Important things to keep in mind as you do this activity:

- Privileges should be age and developmentally appropriate.
- Privileges are EARNED not given.
- Privileges are never negotiated.
- Expected behaviors should be reasonable, age and developmentally appropriate.
- Expected behaviors should be known.
- Consequences should be earned based on behavior demonstrated.
- Consequences are based on choices the person made, therefore because of their choice and their behavior, they earned the outcome.
- Everyone should be encouraged to make choices in their own best interest, and be reminded they can do this.
- When the parent (person who is supposed to be mature and owning the responsibility for structure enforcement) evaluates the behavior, they should keep in mind:
    o Being reasonable, logical and unemotional.
    o Being consistent.
    o Using the IF…..THEN…. as the rule for behavior.
    o Reminding that the person is responsible for their decisions and choices.
    o Setting the limit, defining it, and then they stand by that limit (over and over and over and over).
    o NO means NO.
    o They should be prepared to that this may go on for a while, and they need to stand firm and not budge as long as it is reasonable.
    o It is appropriate to tell someone that their behavior is unacceptable or inappropriate.
    o Don't try to reason or logic with someone who is highly emotional, they are not able to hear what you are saying. That is why your behavior (standing firmly and staying firm) is so important.

Activity: Defining Expectations and Consequences Worksheet

Expected Behaviors – IF….	Consequences (outcome) – THEN…

Now, go on and think about these lists as you work through the family contract.

Family Contract

Related to scheduled activities and obligations, what time is expected that I will:
- Get up for school/work:
- Have a healthy breakfast:
- Eat with the family
- Clean their room
- Do assigned chores (please list what and when):
- Shower and take care of grooming/hygiene/self-care
- Go to bed at:
- OTHER:

Related to healthy choices and lifestyle patterns, the following structure is in place:
- No smoking, drinking, or using any form of illegal or nonprescribed substances that alter thinking or mood
- Nutrition should consist of three healthy and balanced meals daily and snacks
- Self-destructive thoughts, behaviors and impulses should be discussed with parents.
- Self-destructive behaviors must be disclosed to parents
- It is reasonable that if social peers are also unhealthy, that parents limit time spent with them to supervised and in home only
- If medications are prescribed, taking them as prescribed is recommended. Honest discussion with physician should occur if there are concerns.
- No cell phones, computer, or other form of communication with peers after _____ pm
- For adolescents: No dating or sexual activities with strangers, while under the influence, put you at risk for being raped/assaulted or with adults, adults being defined as individuals who are over 18 &/or more than 5 years older than a teen
- For adults: No dating or sexual activities with strangers, while under the influence, put you at risk for being raped/assaulted
- No aggression, violence, threatening or coercion allowed
- Supervision of computer usage by responsible adults
- Other:

Related to self-destructive thoughts, behaviors and impulses:
- The main reasons I use self-injury or self-destructive behaviors are:

- I am most likely to engage in self-destructive behaviors when:

- If I have self-destructive thoughts or impulses, I agree to tell my parents. Here is what I will say:

- Here is what would be helpful for them to say or do:

- If I have self-destructive thoughts or impulses, I will do the following:

- I understand, and my parents understand, that by talking about hurting myself, it is not the same as failing, as doing the behavior or relapsing.

- I understand that if I engage in self-injury or self-destructive behaviors that I am showing that I can not manage my feelings, express myself appropriately or ask for attention in healthy ways. Logical consequences of choosing to engage in these behaviors would be:

- If I chose to engage in self-destructive behaviors, I agree to tell my parents/family. And accept the structure they feel is appropriate to help keep me safe, until they know I am safe, and until I demonstrate that I can be safe. How we agree to do this is:

- When I self-injure or act in self-destructive ways, what I need my parents/family to do is:

- If I do not engage in self-injury or self-destructive behavior for _____, I want my family to think about allowing me to:

- They increase structure such as _____ until I can demonstrate I can be safe

- I can demonstrate I am safe by (behaving how?)

Related to self-expression and presentation (dress, hygiene, grooming):
- I am expected to be clean, wear clean and appropriate clothing
- I will not tattoo, pierce, carve, shave, dye, or use excessive make-up or hairstyles or otherwise change my appearance to be provocative and go against my family values or standards. As long as I struggle with being able to keep myself safe, these actions are not considered self-expression or self-definition, they are considered hiding, masking my true feelings and my true self. They are considered provocative and acting out.
- I will not be allowed to dress in sexually provocative ways, or dress older than I am (for teens), or younger than is appropriate for my age.
- I will not hide behind my appearance.
- Final dress code will be defined by parents (with therapist assistance if needed).
- I can:

Related to obligations/responsibilities:
- I understand that I am expected to attend school/work as my first priority after my health
- I understand that my social obligations, team/sports obligations are secondary to my school and work obligations
- If I am unable to take care of my health and my safety and the basic obligations, it shows that I am unable to manage myself in other areas of my life
- If I am unable to manage my health and safety, my parents will:
  Example: Supervise my visits with my friends: (who is and is not allowed)

  Supervise my time on the computer: (what is and is not allowed)

  Supervise or only me on the phone/cell phone under these conditions:

- How can I earn trust back to my parents?

Review the list of Expected Behaviors and Consequences Worksheet. Define the list of expected behaviors and the consequences that will be earned as a result of these decisions.

We expect (IF….)	The consequence (THEN)….

In this family, we value_____, and show that we value this when we (behave):

_This will be reviewed on:_____

Any serious disagreements will be mediated by the therapist, at the next scheduled appointment. Until that time, since safety, consistency and health are the most important, all behavior and decisions will be made with that foundation.

I agree to follow these guidelines and rules:

_Name_____

_Date:_____

_Name_____

_Date:_____

_Name_____

_Date:_____

Unhealthy and Destructive Attitudes and Beliefs

Ok, don't take this list too seriously, but think seriously about if you believe or practice any of these. If you do, you may want to reconsider the impact these beliefs have on your family and the person who is self-destructive behaviors and thinking.

How not to be healthy: How to feed and grow self-injury & self-destruction

Here it is a simple recipe for families who want their children <u>to not be healthy</u>:

- Have conflict where there has to be a winner or loser, fight like your life depends on it.
- Keep changing the rules.
- Give in when their argument is aggressive.
- Change the rules so that the kid is happy and at least not fighting with you.
- Give in when there are threats.
- Don't do it (whatever it is) because it is inconvenient and uncomfortable.
- Tell them to "suck it up" and "stop being weak."
- Criticize constantly, especially about their weight, how they look like someone you don't like, compare them to some crazy person.
- Drink, take drugs, act aggressively, do whatever you want, you're a grown up - but they better not do what you do!!
- Constantly challenge the therapist or doctor, demand to know constantly why therapy isn't working.
- Take the position that "it's not my problem," that the kid is the one with the problem.
- Challenge them to go ahead and commit suicide or cut themselves to shreds.
- Hey I wish I had to eat a menu like that, I think I'll go on a diet.
- Fast food is easier, who cares, at least I'm giving you food.
- He's just expressing himself, so what if he threatened the teacher, the guys an idiot anyway.
- Blame everyone.
- Drink before you pick up your kid for therapy.
- Go bar hopping and share your stash with your kid.
- Have unrealistic expectations of perfection for your kid.
- Believe the worst about your kid.
- Let them be on their computer all the time, hey, at least they are out of your hair.
- Be afraid of everything, belief the person who self-injures can't manage anything.
- Don't talk about anything, keep family secrets.
- Don't let the person who self-injures have any privacy.
- Let your new spouse/other adult live in the house, but don't expect them to participate as a role model.
- Don't go to therapy with them, don't talk to the therapist.
- Let your kid date older people, at least they're responsible.
- Believe and act like it is your job to make your kid happy.
- Don't consider changing anything in your home, it's your kids' problem anyway.
- Don't expect all the adults living in your house to act like healthy adults.

- Tell your kid how much money they are costing you.
- Allow your kid to sleep through therapy or not go to school because it is easier than fighting with them.
- Have no standards for self-respect and appropriate appearance and behavior, after all, they are just expressing themselves.
- Go ahead, who cares if they are tattooed, shaved, carved, wearing all black, dyed hair, etc. What do they have to do to get your attention and your expectations that they manage themselves in age-appropriate ways?
- Don't worry that your drugs, drinking, eating disorder could at all affect your kids.
- Make your kid the adult of the family – she has to learn how to do the bills some day.
- Excuse inappropriate behavior because of fear that the person will act out more.

Okay, okay, these are extreme. I wish they were just things I made up as I was writing this section. Sadly, I've heard these hundreds of times. Just ask any therapist or counselor, and their eyes will become sad and they'll tell you the number of families they've worked with, and the things they've heard said, and heard about being practiced.

Activity: Unhealthy and Healthy Attitudes
On the next page is an activity for you to complete. Think about these unhealthy attitudes and your reaction to them. Also consider, and discuss, do any of these exist in your family? What are the effects of these attitudes and beliefs?

What is a healthier attitude or rule? What value does this healthier attitude reflect? If you consider what a child/teen needs to become a healthier person who can manage demands of life, do your attitudes and practices help instill and teach?

Change these to healthier thoughts, beliefs or standards. What is the value you want to connect to each? As a family you should discuss these and be honest about whether or not these are practiced in your home and in your relationships.

Unhealthy Attitude	Healthier attitude	Your Family Value
Have conflict where there has to be a winner or loser, fight like your life depends on it		
Keep changing the rules		
Give in when their argument is aggressive		

Unhealthy Attitude	Healthier attitude	Your Family Value
Give in when there are threats		
Don't do it (whatever it is) because it is inconvenient and uncomfortable		
Tell them to "suck it up" and "stop being weak"		
Criticize constantly, especially about their weight, how they look like someone you don't like, compare them to some crazy person		
Drink, take drugs, act aggressively, do whatever you want, you're a grown up - but they better not do what you do!!		
Constantly challenge the therapist or doctor, demand to know constantly why therapy isn't working		
Take the position that "it's not my problem," that the kid is the one with the problem		
Challenge them to go ahead and commit suicide or cut themselves to shreds		
Hey I wish I had to eat a menu like that, I think I'll go on a diet		
Fast food is easier, who cares, at least I'm giving you food		

Unhealthy Attitude	Healthier attitude	Your Family Value
He's just expressing himself, so what if he threatened the teacher, the guys an idiot anyway		
Blame everyone else for the problems		
Drink before you pick up your kid for therapy		
Go bar hopping and share your stash with your kid		
Have unrealistic expectations of perfection for your kid		
Believe the worst about your kid		
Let them be on their computer all the time, hey, at least they are out of your hair		
Be afraid of everything, belief the person who self-injures can't manage anything		
Don't talk about anything, keep family secrets		
Don't let the person who self-injures have any privacy		

Unhealthy Attitude	Healthier attitude	Your Family Value
Let your new spouse/other adult live in the house, but don't expect them to participate as a role model		
Don't go to therapy with them, don't talk to the therapist		
Let your kid date older people, at least they're responsible		
Believe and act like it is your job to make your kid happy		
Don't consider changing anything in your home, it's your kids problem anyway		
Don't expect all the adults living in your house to act like healthy adults		
Tell your kid how much money they are costing you		
Allow your kid to sleep through therapy or not go to school because it is easier than fighting with them		
Have no standards for self-respect and appropriate appearance and behavior, after all, they are just expressing themselves		
Go ahead, who cares if they are tattooed, shaved, carved, wearing all black, dyed hair, etc.		

What do they have to do to get your attention and your expectations that they manage themselves in age-appropriate ways?		
Don't worry that your drugs, drinking, eating disorder could at all affect your kids		
Make your kid the adult of the family – she has to learn how to do the bills some day		
Excuse inappropriate behavior because of fear that the person will act out more		
Your thoughts!		

Activity: Identify Your Family's Attitudes or Beliefs

Now think about your own family's attitudes or beliefs. Each person should offer some ideas they think are unhealthy, and offer suggestions for healthier attitudes. These healthier attitudes should be connected to at least on Family Value.

Unhealthy Attitude	Healthier attitude	In this family we value or believe

---

Purpose = Reason, aim, goal, target, meaning
- What is the purpose of Family? What does your family stand for, why have a family, what did you want? What do you want to create? What do you want to teach your children?
- What do you stand for as a family? How do you create that?

The purpose of life is a life of purpose. <u>Robert Byrne</u>

Activity: Creating Purpose and Direction for Your Family ....
1. Set a destination. What do you want for your family?

Without goals, and plans to reach them, you are like a ship that has set sail with no destination. Fitzhugh Dodson

---

2. What is something that is necessary to change to create this?

Start by doing what's necessary, then what's possible, and suddenly you are doing the impossible. Francis of Assisi

---

3. What are you willing to do differently to make this happen because you believe it is important?

---

4. Why change now?

If not us, who? If not now, when? John F. Kennedy

5. What skills or resources do we have that will help us be able?

They are able because they think they are able. Virgil

6. What is the hardest thing for each one of us to accept about all of this?

We all have ability. The difference is how we use it. Stevie Wonder

Activity: What I Want You to Know About Me

What is important to tell your family about you? How did you develop your values, your personality style or your habits? How do they work for you? How is your family important to you? What do you want or need from them? What are you willing to do differently? What aren't you willing to do? What do I want to teach you about the experiences in my life?

Was I honest? Why or why not?

Activity: Taking Our Family Inventory

Every family has some strengths and some limitations. Some have resources and other things are missing or needed. It is helpful to consider what these are as you begin to think about the process of changing and about building more structure in your family. You may be surprised at how rich you may actually be – people can be far more able, skillful, and willing than we know!

For each person in your household, think about them in terms of their age, maturity, and what skills and abilities they possess and what they can offer to help the family as a whole work.

Name:	What skills and abilities do they have?	How they can help

Name:	What skills and abilities do they have?	How they can help

Name:	What skills and abilities do they have?	How they can help

Name:	What skills and abilities do they have?	How they can help

Name:	What skills and abilities do they have?	How they can help

Activity: Identifying a Problem and Creating Possible Solutions

Name a problem situation in the family:	What would help make this situation better? Who would need to do what to help this happen?
People yelling and not listening to each other	

Activity: What limitations, problems or weaknesses do we need help with to be healthier?

Who is not good at what?	What does that person need	Who could help?
Zed Cleaning up and organizing	Help keeping the house neat Teaching him to pick up after himself, having to earn back items he leaves all over the house	Zoey, mom, EVERYBODY

Activity: Understanding Purpose of Self-Destructive Behaviors

Each member of the family should consider the following questions. Believe it or not, you have choices about the behaviors you do, even the self-destructive ones. Everyone has some behaviors that are not necessarily healthy. Think of why you have used self-destructive behaviors. List them. In the next column, think of at least two other healthier things you are willing to try.

What are the unhealthy or less than healthy behaviors do you do?

Why I choose to use these behaviors	Other healthier things I'm willing to try

Pick one healthier behavior that you will practice for a day. When can you try it?

One can choose to go back toward safety or forward toward growth. Growth must be chosen again and again; fear must be overcome again and again. Abraham Maslow

One this page, draw the life line of your family, and the lessons you've learned about life. Think about how they have made each of you the person you are today. What are the important lessons?

Activity: Our Personal Family Crest

Try not to become a man of success but a man of value. Albert Einstein

This is your Crest. Your personal family crest represents important aspects of your family as a whole. Each part of the Crest represents something different about you. Use words, symbols, colors, pictures. Left side, going down is 1, 2 & 3 and right side going down, 4, 5, & 6

1	What gives your family strength	4	What skills your family has
2	Things that are important to your family	5	In our family, we….
3	Symbols that represent each of you	6	Symbol that represents your family

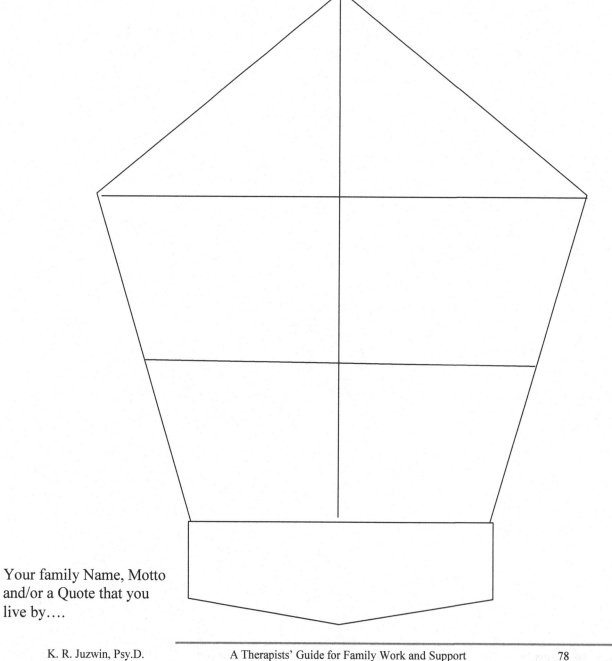

Your family Name, Motto and/or a Quote that you live by….

Activity: Our Family Creed

So long as there is breath in me, that long I will persist. For now I know one of the greatest principles on success; if I persist long enough I will win. Og Mandino

It is important to know what your family stands for and believes is important. These are your operating rules and that are your family "blueprint" for living. In this exercise, think about these and write your family rules:

We as a family, we believe:

The rules for relationships with each other:

What is important to each one of us, and how each of us will practice this? (One of each of you.)

What about friends?

We tend to socialize with people who we see as having something in common with us in terms of interests, values and to some extent, experiences and behaviors. However, there is more to it that just this. We tend to socialize with people who accept us and have similar behaviors. While needing friends and a social group is a necessary part of every stage of life, it is often the case that adolescents who self-injure may tend to seek out and form relationships with others who are like them or support the self-injury and suicidal thinking (Joiner, 2003) and other self-destructive behaviors.

Remember, friends just don't happen face-to-face anymore. With the electronic generation or the "e-kid" generation, teens and children are constantly communicating with other people either on the phone, texting, or online social networking. It is common place to see people together, yet they are on their cells or electronic equipment texting, talking, or whatever with someone who is not there. Multiple conversations going on at the same time is becoming the norm. Many times we carry these conversations on without awareness that other people are even around us. This is called being disconnected and unaware.

There is little concern for our impact on others around us, because we teach our children that they don't have consequences for their decisions and that their behavior is acceptable. Many of our children/teens/young adults do not self-monitor because of lack of structure and not being taught cause and effect. Increasingly, parents are often on their phone as well. So it isn't uncommon to drive by a family and observe that some of them are hooked into a video, some on a handheld game, while others are on their phones. None of them are interacting. This is an opportunity that is missed for family conversation and discussion.

Many of these kids have relationships that have never met *face to face*. As a result of these relationships, there are many risks, including:

- Online suicide and "cutting" clubs.
- Increased sexual conversation "sexting", highly sexualized photos.
- Increased bullying.
- No longer do individuals have fights with each other, now it is network against network.
- Decreased ability to resolve or settle conflicts face to face.
- Cyber bullying.
- Lack of respect of boundaries, leaving messages, communicating regardless of where they are, what time of day, etc.
- Changing social norms, i.e., texting while at the dinner table, with while with friends/family, in school, etc. Acceptable to make/receive calls whenever, without restriction.
- Increased entitlement that they are owed a computer, without supervision, as well as a phone to be used at their discretion.
- Decreased supervision from adults regarding social appropriateness and developmentally and maturationally appropriate relationships so they get involved in inappropriate relationships.

- Once something is sent out into cyber space, who knows how long it is going to last and where it is going and to whom.
- Social networks can be like snowballs rolling down hill, building and building.
- Decreased age-appropriate verbal social skills.
- Decreased ability to read social cues (remember online and texting, there are no social cues).
- Decreased ability to read and understand verbal and face-to-face social cues.
- Inability to delay gratification, tolerate frustration.
- Lack of accountability for their words and actions.
- People text or email without scanning or thinking clearly about how the message will be received.
- It is much easier to send e-messages that have very hurtful, destructive and provocative materials because they don't have to be there when the message is read and reacted to by the recipient.
- Additionally parents often have little awareness of the content of what is being posted and exchanged and with WHO their kids are interacting.
- Lack of learning about the effects of what their words can mean directly.
- Before e-conversations, if we were mad at someone, we had to look them in the eye and be face to face for a good part of the situation. Your brain is programmed to read social cues and understand tones in words. This is how you learn about relationships, managing your feelings and making things right or settling something. This is the foundation of human relationships.
- You or the other person showed your feelings on your face, in your body language and in your voice. This gives critical cues about human feelings and reactions. No electronic device will ever capture and teach those important lessons.

Activity: Define the rules for healthy friends and relationships

---

A brief word on SELF-EXPRESSION

Every one should have the ability to express him or herself. We do this is several ways: our language, dress and mannerisms. If you have someone who is expressing his or herself using unhealthy behavior, then you as a responsible and reasonable parent need to step in. This means getting involved and setting limits on behaviors that are:

> Unhealthy (self-destruction, damaging skin, drugs, nutrition, purging, isolation)
> Unsafe (sexually promiscuous, fighting/bullying, dangerous, online relationships)
> Age-inappropriate (sexual expression, acting out, dating people significantly older)
> Provocative (inappropriate make-up, hair, clothing)

A brief word on SELF-DEFINITION versus SELF-ESTEEM

Self-definition is the way we describe ourselves. It involves the way we speak about and the terms we use to describe ourselves. It is different than self-esteem, because this implies a subjective value or statement of worth. The reality is self-esteem is arbitrary and often not based in reality. It tends to be more a statement about what we are willing to believe about ourselves and what we say about ourselves. This self-talk tends to create the set of rules about a why life seems so random and out of our control. This self-talk also sets the stage for creating more negatively and self-fulfilling prophecies. This means, "I am a piece of garbage, so why would I think I am smart; see I failed this test, I'm stupid," is typically supported by a string of failures in school. This isn't the kid who will prove someone wrong about "how dumb they are." It often is used to avoid being responsible for actions, making healthy choices or taking risks in life. How many times do you hear, "if she had better self-esteem, she'd….." as a reason why people don't do things. Identity is about definition, not about an arbitrary sense of worth or lack thereof.

In consideration of self-injury and self-destructive behaviors, the idea of self-definition allows someone to use many different words and ideas to define themselves. It allows for a long list of definitions and descriptions. It is important to avoid arguments about the "worth" someone has; no one wins that argument.

Self-Expression and Individuality

There are a lot of ways to express ourselves, and individuality is important. What is important to know about kids who self-injure is that their self-expression is sending mixed messages:

> I'm going to make myself look as despicable and self-loathing as I feel, but you better not judge me.
> I'm trying to keep you away, why don't you like me.
> See everyone thinks I'm a freak, why doesn't any one like me.
> I'm really tough, stay away, you might hurt me.
> I try to be perfect, but if you really knew me, you would see how flawed I am.
> If I'm nice to everyone, then I have value.
> If I'm such a freak, then I can't disappoint anyone or be hurt by anyone.
> If I'm thin, then people will think I'm like them, "normal."

This is one of those opportunities to help with age-appropriate self-definition. Remember, tattoo's and piercings may have lifelong implications. The same goes for drug and alcohol abuse, smoking, sexual promiscuity, restricting, binge/purging behaviors and self-injury. Some behaviors have consequences you can't undo. For those kids struggling with self-definition, allowing them to hide behind an extreme role or demeanor may not be helpful. *If they are engaging in self-destructive and/or a dangerous life-style (which anorexia, drug abuse and promiscuous socializing/sex is included), then this is not a case of self-expression.*

It is reasonable to set limits on what you think is acceptable or not acceptable in terms of self-expression. If your kid is engaging in self-destructive behaviors, allowing them to use extreme dress styles, make-up, hair, piercings or overly sexualized or provocative clothing is not helping them learn to self-manage. They create a persona that is an effort to communicate their struggles and attempts to manage. *What you are doing is allowing them to externalize their emotions, which causes them to not have to develop self-definition internally.* When someone is able to manage themselves safely and in a healthy and age-appropriate way, *then* they have learned how to self-manage, and expressing themselves through clothes, dress, hair, etc., is a different issue. This is one of "this is who I am." For the kid who can't manage, these extreme presentations mask who they really are inside. You want your child/teen to have an identity before they create a role, image or mask to hide behind.

Why your self-injuring kid needs these limits, boundaries & expectations

Your kid needs you to expect that they take care of themselves and to behave and present themselves in a socially acceptable manner. Why?

- Parents state the rules, and uphold them. The kid struggles against them. This is an age-old and very necessary struggle. Removing this struggle, because it is easier, or because you believe it is unnecessary, denies your child an important life lesson and developmental milestone.
- This reinforces expectations for being healthy and making good choices.
- This reinforces family values.
- It gives the kid an opportunity to problem solve, tolerate frustration and demonstrate maturity, and to earn trust and respect of their parents.
- The developmental milestone here is just as important as those in infancy and early childhood, and prepares them to be able to manage the next phase of life, young adulthood.

It teaches:

- The importance of self-respect.
- The importance of appropriate and direct expression.
- The importance of using words (language) to get needs met and to express oneself.
- The importance of controlling behavior, so that you don't behave in a way that you can't take back or fix.
- The importance of tolerating frustration.
- The importance of knowing and respecting limits and authority.
- Problem-solving, conflict management and resolution.

- The importance of learning that you can't always get what you want or act like you want and get away with it.
- You don't have to have relationships based on unhealthy behaviors to get accepted.
- That being healthy, mature and age-appropriate may get you closer to independence.
- When someone behaves in unhealthy, immature or age-inappropriate ways, such as using self-destructive or dangerous behaviors, they are not able to manage themselves independently, and consequently may need more structure, attention and supervision.
- Every conversation with your child is an opportunity to teach them about:
    o How to have relationships.
    o How to manage relationships.
    o How to recognize respect, trust and healthy relationships.
    o How to recognize disrespect, distrust and unhealthy relationships.
    o Encouragement, problem-solving, and socializing.
    o Your values.
    o Boundaries.
    o Limits.
    o True support and helpfulness.
    o Healthy rules, boundaries and expectations.
    o Practicing what you preach.
    o Modeling for them how to be a person.

Activity: What are rules of healthy relationships?

Compare your rules to your parents:

Yours	Your Parents

What are the areas you disagree? How will you resolve this?

What are the areas you agree?

Why is this important to discuss?

What are the lessons you want to teach each other about relationships that are important?

Activity: Communicating Important Thoughts & Opinions

PARENTS: please answer based on what you think is important.

Goals of parenting (what I want for my children):

1.
2.
3.

What worries me the most for my child/ren in their life/lives:

1.
2.
3.

What I don't want my kids to learn the hard way (or the way you had to):

1.
2.
3.

How I show love and responsible parenting for my children:

1.
2.
3.

Things I think my child/ren are worried about or would say are stressful to them:

1.
2.
3.
4.
5.

Things about being a parent that scares me:
1.
2.
3.
4.

What will have to change about our family life so things will be different:
1.
2.
3.
4.
5.

Ask your kids their opinions about your answers. Discuss this as a family.

KIDS: please answer the questions based on what you think is important.

Goals of parenting (what I think the goals of being a parent are):
1.
2.
3.

What you think your parents worry about most for/about you:

1.
2.
3.

What your parents are afraid you are going to learn the hard way:
1.
2.
3.

How parents show love and responsible parenting for their children:

1.
2.
3.

Values that are important for a family to have so everyone is healthy:

1.
2.
3.

Things I think my parents are worried about or would say are stressful to them:
1.
2.
3.
4.
5.

Things about being a teenager that scare me:
1.
2.
3.

What will have to change about our family life so things will be different:
1.
2.
3.
4.
5.

References

Andover, M. S., Pepper, C. M., Ryabchenko, K. A., Orrico, E. G., & Gibb, B. E. (2005). Self-mutilation and symptoms of depression, anxiety, and borderline personality disorder. *Suicide and Life-Threatening Behavior, 35*, 581-591.

Bennewith, O., Stocks, N., Gunnell, D., Peters, T. J., Evans, M. O., & Sharp, D. J. (2002). General practice based intervention to prevent repeat episodes of deliberate self harm. *BMJ: British Medical Journal, 1254*, 324-328.

Brown, M. Z., Comtois, K. A., & Linehan, M. M. (2002). Reasons for suicide attempts and nonsuicidal self-injury in women with borderline personality disorder. *Journal of Abnormal Psychology, 111*, 198-202.

Chitsabesan, P., Harrington, R., Harrington, V., & Tomenson, B. (2003). Predicting repeat self-harm in children--how accurate can we expect to be? *European Child and Adolescent Psychiatry, 12*, 23-29.

Gratz, K. L. (2001). Measurement of deliberate self-harm: Preliminary data on the Deliberate Self-Harm Inventory. *Journal of Psychopathology and Behavioral Assessment, 23*, 253-263.

Gratz, K. L. (2006). Risk factors for deliberate self-harm among female college students: The role and interaction of childhood maltreatment, emotional inexpressivity, and affect intensity/reactivity. *American Journal of Orthopsychiatry, 76*, 238-250.

Hurry, J. (2000). Deliberate self-harm in children and adolescents. *International Review of Psychiatry, 12*, 31-36.

Isacsson, G., & Rich, C. L. (2001). Management of patients who deliberately harm themselves. *BMJ: British Medical Journal, 322*, 213-215.

Jacobson, C. M. & Gould, M. (2007). The epidemiology and phenomenology of non-suicidal self-injurious behavior among adolescents: a critical review of the literature. *Archives of Suicide Research, 11*, 129-147.

Joiner, T. E., Jr. (2003). Contagion of suicidal symptoms as a function of assortative relating and shared relationship stress in college roommates. *Journal of Adolescence, 26*, 495-504.

Klonsky, E. D. & Meuhlenkamp, J. J. 2007. Self-injury: a research review for the practitioner. *Journal of Clinical Psychology, 63, 1045-56.*

Lloyd-Richardson, E. E., Perrine, N., Dierker, L. & Kelly, M. L. (2007). Characteristics and functions of non-suicidal self-injury in a community sample of adolescents. *Psychological Medicine, 37,* 1183-1192.

Nock, M. K. & Cha, C. B. (2009). Psychological models of Nonsuicidal self-injury, Understanding Nonsuicidal self-injury: origins, assessment, and treatment, Nock, M.K., (ed). Washington, D. C.: American Psychological Association.

Nock, M. K., Holmberg, E. B., Photos, V. I., & Michel, B. D. (2007). Self-injurious thoughts and behaviors interview: development, reliability, and validity in an adolescent sample. *Psychological Assessment, 19,* 309-317.

Nock, M. K., & Kessler, R. C. (2006). Prevalence of and risk factors for suicide attempts versus suicide gestures: analysis of the National Comorbidity Survey. *Journal of Abnormal Psychology, 115*, 616-623.

Nock, M. K. & Mendes, W. B. (2008). Physiological arousal, distress tolerance, and social problem-solving deficits among adolescent's self-injurers. *Journal of Consulting and Clinical Psychology, 76,* 26-38.

Nock, M. K., & Prinstein, M. J. (2004). A functional approach to the assessment of self-mutilative behavior. *Journal of Consulting and Clinical Psychology, 72,* 885-890.

Nock, M. K., & Prinstein, M. J. (2005). Clinical features and behavioral functions of adolescent self-mutilation. *Journal of Abnormal Psychology, 114,* 140-146.

Ross, S., Heath, N. & Toste, J. R. (2008). Non-suicidal self-injury and eating pathology in high school students. *American Journal of Orthopsychiatry, 1,* 83-92.

Suyemoto, K. L. (1998). The functions of self-mutilation. *Clinical Psychology Review, 18,* 531-554.

Whitlock, J., Eckenrode, J., & Silverman, D. (2006). Self-injurious behaviors in a college population. *Pediatrics, 117,* 1939-1948.